Magic Wool

Magic Wool

Creative Pictures and Tableux with Natural Sheep's Wool

Dagmar Schmidt and Freya Jaffke

Floris Books

Translated by Donald Maclean

Photographs by Wolpert & Strehle, Fotodesign, Stuttgart

First published in German in 1993 under
the title *Gestalten mit farbiger Wolle* by
Verlag Freies Geistesleben GmbH, Stuttgart
First published in English in 2000 by Floris Books
This edition published in 2011

British Library CIP Data available
ISBN 978-086315-829-2
Printed in China

Contents

Foreword

For many years fairy-tale figures made from unspun wool have been an integral part of craft activities in Waldorf schools. Over the course of time, a wealth of information has been collected about the craft, and many courses have been run on the subject. As a result of the constant demand for further information this book has been compiled to answer these questions, and as an introduction for those who do not know about these kinds of figures.

This book has been written as a result of my experience as a craft teacher with Freya Jaffke, whose work with coloured wool stems from teaching in Waldorf kindergartens.

Dagmar Schmidt

Pictures and Figures
with Magic Wool

by Dagmar Schmidt

Introduction

The enchantment of fairy-tale wool figures lies in the soft unconstricted forms and the delicate, yet living colours obtained by layering techniques. Plant-dyed wool is especially suitable for our purpose. Even strong plant dyes are still quite subtle. As you create a picture, the difference between chemical and plant dyes becomes clear. But we should not discount chemically-dyed wool. Powerful colours, properly applied, can enliven a picture. Plant-dyed wool can help children especially to develop a fine sense of colour, not only in their creating, but also in observing a picture, because of the subtle nuances of the different shades of colour.

Coloured unspun wool is sometimes called 'magic wool,' indicating a material which is loose enough for creating fanciful figures, particularly suitable for a child's imagination.

Materials

THE BASE

For a background use stiff cloth, felt or a rough woven material such as hessian, to which wool will stick. If necessary, this base can be roughened up further with a stiff brush. Choose the right colour for the scene. For example, a night scene should use mid or dark blue; an indoor scene for the twelve fairies surrounding the cradle of Brier Rose requires a light, warm background, such as beige. Rumpelstiltskin can be created on red felt as he is spinning straw into gold, though the colour should not be too glaring.

Once the picture is finished the layers of wool are often so thick that hardly anything can be seen of the background, and it only faintly shimmers through. Nevertheless, it can enhance the composition.

THE WOOL

Unspun wool has different textures and fibres depending on the type of sheep that it comes from, for instance, there are long, short-haired or curly types of wool. Long-haired ewe's wool is the best. In general, carded (that is, combed), long-haired wool is preferable, as this can be teased into fine, even and unknotted wool. Larger areas can be created with this kind of wool and it is the easiest to work with. However, short-haired, badly carded wool with knots in it, can also be used at times; it depends on what is to be depicted. Even curly wool can be useful.

Ideally, have at least two, or even three, different shades of each colour. In addition to red, orange, yellow, green, blue, brown, violet and pink, there are also a range of skin colours, suitable for faces, hands etc., and off-white.

In fairy-tale pictures, blue, green and yellow shades are used more frequently than red, pink or orange, so you should have more of these colours to hand for forest scenes, sky, background and carpets.

To create a wool picture you will need:

> Felt or a rough or woollen material
>   background
> Coloured unspun wool
> An iron
> Smooth paper (tissue paper is best)
> Two wooden rods, longer than the
>   width of the picture
> Darning needle
> Woollen yarn

Laying out a wool picture

Seeing a wool picture for the first time, people are primarily interested in how the wool sticks to the base without being glued or sewn on.

This is achieved by applying the wool in very fine, thin layers which cling together because of the nature of the fibre. This clinging together is so strong that, when it is finished, it is possible to detach the whole picture from the background without spoiling it.

To start a picture, lay the base material on a table. Take a tuft of wool, hold it to the base, press one end of it on to the base with one hand (or with one or two fingers), and pull it out in the desired direction with the other hand, always leaving some wool free, as with spinning (see Figures 1 to 4).

To represent a person or, for instance, a shepherd (see Figures 5 to 8), lay a thin layer of wool on to the base to represent the head. Then, while holding the tuft at the neck press one end on to the base and pull it down with the other hand, so that an initial thin layer is created. Repeat this process – laying, pressing down and pulling out – until the figure takes shape. Each fine layer is laid upon the one before and pressed down, and in this way the whole area is gradually covered and the composition of the picture delicately revealed. At the beginning, it is advisable not to concentrate too much on details, but to keep the whole picture in mind, allowing it to slowly emerge.

If the wool layers have become very thick in certain places, and you still wish to press on

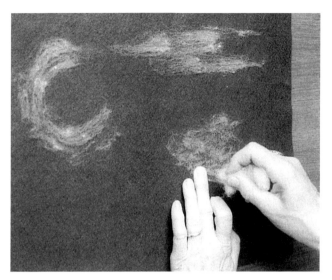

1

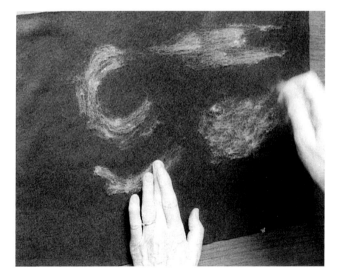

2

more colours, you can pass a steam iron over them, or lay a thin piece of paper over the wool,

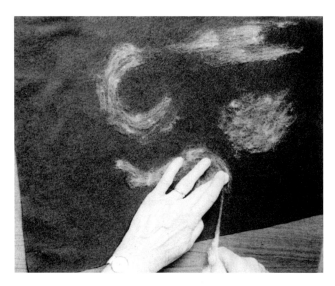

3

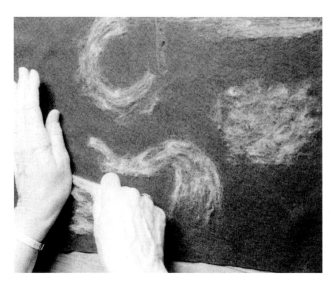

4

then a damp cloth and use an ordinary iron. In this way the wool is compressed and matted, and you can easily correct any wrong outlines after ironing. Wiping and rubbing out is not necessary here, for at any time wool can be removed or laid differently. A little pressure with a finger in this or that direction is all that is needed, and the whole thing takes on a different appearance.

If you have got so far that you consider that the picture is finished then you can iron it again, but this time on the back. To do this lay the picture face down on a sheet of smooth paper, on which the wool will not catch, and run the iron lightly over the back (do not leave the iron on it). Then gently steam iron the front, so that the iron is applied lightly to certain spots, and pressed down more firmly in others. In this way you can give texture to the figures and trees which have been created by the layering. Pictures are most successful when wool layers are applied as thinly as possible throughout the creative process. This is often overlooked by beginners.

If you wish, you can sew the picture layers on to the base using running stitch. Make the single stitches as small as possible, just big enough to secure the wool, not quite pricked through the material and 5 cm (2 in) apart, similar to sewing an invisible seam.

The wool picture can then be secured, and reinforced above and below by a wooden rod, which makes it easier to hang it up. Sew the base material on to the rods with woollen yarn (in a colour matching the picture) using stitches that are not too tight. You can easily detach the picture layer at the top and bottom edges and press it back on again.

5

6

7

8

Do not use a fixed frame or glass, as this reduces its characteristic charm. Wool absorbs a lot of light, so the picture should be hung in a bright place. The best effect is with the light coming from the side.

Some advice for creating pictures

Practical hints

Once you have learned the basic skill of layering wool pictures, you can develop other pictures, according to the time of year or an approaching festival. With fairy-tale pictures, take care not to present a particular scene too rigidly, but allow children's imagination plenty of scope to fill in the details themselves. Avoid hard outlines even with lifeless objects such as chairs, tables or houses. People's gestures and animals can be clearly represented and differentiated. Intangible things such as moods and conversations can be expressed through colour.

What should we take particular care of when forming wool shapes?

1. Where possible the wool picture should be started in daylight, as artificial light can alter the colours.
2. The base should be big enough. For instance, a Star Thaler (page 23) only needs a small area of 40 x 30 cm (16 x 12 in). If you want to present more people, animals, fairies or gnomes, then you will need an area of at least 55 x 45 cm (22 x 18 in).
3. Pull or tease the wool so that, for example, still water is horizontal; running water flows or ripples; a tree grows from the roots up towards the branches; or depending on the weather, a sky is horizontal and calm, cloudy or with sunbeams shining all around.

4. The main scene should be as large and recognizable as possible, with the surroundings only indicated by the colours (see the Twelve Fairies on page 20 or the forest background on page 23).
5. Human features should not be detailed.
6. If you wish to make a larger single-coloured area more vivid, you can make the base with bright colours. Then lay a pastel shade over it so that the brightly coloured wool softly shines through (see Cinderella, page 28).

Good advice, however, cannot replace real practice, which you will only get while working with the material. As you build up the fine wool layers you will notice the difference between light-coloured on dark wool, and dark-coloured on light wool. If the base is a light colour, the wool itself will create shadows when the light falls on it. This can be avoided by initially covering a bright base with a similar coloured wool.

A picture gives a balanced effect when it contains a broad range of basic colours, though they do not all need to be bright.

A blue base is suitable for many pictures.

Care

With good care a wool picture will last many years. Make sure that the picture does not hang in a draught, otherwise the wool will eventually come away from the base. Keep an eye on this from time to time; you can gently press the wool back on by moving the palm of your hand upwards. Above all do not let it flap about, and keep it out of the reach of very small children.

Sometimes wool has to be protected against moths. If it hangs in a bright airy room it is less likely to be affected. Little discs of cedar or juniper wood attached behind are sufficient. If the picture is to be stored away for a longer period, lavender oil is a natural product, and its scent drives moths away.

To store, wrap the picture in tissue paper and lay it between two sheets of cardboard, or roll it round a tube and pack it well. Both methods will keep it flat for a long time. With a little careful attention, you can correct anything that is out of place, pull out sections that were formerly in relief, and restore the picture to its original condition.

Making wool pictures with children

If an adult is making a wool picture in the presence of children the latter will want to do the same, whether they are three or eight years old. You can give them some felt or whatever is being used: a small easily-managed piece for young children; a bigger piece for older children. At first, just give them the main colours of wool so that they are not confused by the variety. The young children will follow the adult's example and imitate the expert. Let them lay the wool in their own way; each colour on its own or mixed; in order or not; and in this way they can cover their felt. They simply enjoy doing the same as the grown-up. Of course they do not have the same patience and will be finished much sooner.

A five-year-old girl who was present at a course for mothers was influenced by the involvement of the adults with their activity. With great perseverance she laid out her wool picture, and revealed an amazing skill for laying wool, resulting in a harmoniously coloured work without an actual picture. Older children are more conscious of what they are creating and often follow the way in which the adult applies a motif or creates a mood. Children with vivid imaginations soon create independently. You can give them more colours as they require them.

After wool has been introduced to early school-age children, you can make a large wool picture with them. A shepherd with his flock is a very suitable theme. Get each child to carefully tease out a handful of washed but uncarded wool and make a little sheep. Then, the children can put their

9 A wool picture made by a child

sheep (which can be quite simple) on the felt, on which a shepherd (made by the teacher or adult) is already waiting. Children can also take part in making stars, clouds and meadows and so join in creating a beautiful picture. Children become very skilful doing this concentrated work. It is not important for them to create a perfect, completely recognizable image. However, if a picture is to be displayed prominently in a room it is better if it is as beautiful as possible, as these images make a deep impression on young children.

If you wish to make a picture in the presence of children, so that the children can follow the whole process, keep to simple, basic forms and colours, as you will be limited for time, and you will not be able to devote your whole attention to what you are doing. In this instance, the wool will not be so finely layered but laid on more thickly. This makes it easier to break up the picture at a later date, and create a new picture with the same wool. If children are present when you dismantle the picture, do it slowly and carefully so that it does not appear like mindless vandalism.

Using up leftovers

Every activity will leave bits of teased-out wool tufts which cannot be used again. You can collect them and card them again. If you then spin the wool you will have a surprisingly colourful yarn.

Pictures with stories

The Twelve Fairies (Brier Rose)

On a beige background, twelve heads form the basis of the circle in which the fairies stand around the cradle. Then, lay the colour sequence of the robes without appointing specific colours to individual fairies, and use flowing transitions leaving form and colour free. After making the king, queen and cradle, loosely cover the whole background and foreground with a thin a layer of wool, so that the felt underlay is evenly covered. Check that you are happy with the overall composition, and make any necessary adjustments.

Now the colours can be made more intense by applying more layers: first, the fairies standing at the back (yellow, green, blue); then, the fairies at the front (red, pink). Draw the wool upwards

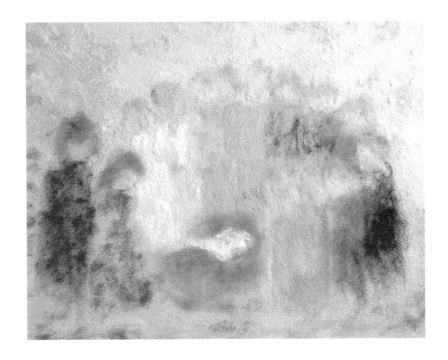

10 The basic composition

to make a clean finish. Faces and hands can be given more detail, and the queen, king and cradle can be made clearer. Next, the remaining areas can have their colours finalized. Then check the overall appearance again.

If the colour and form of the composition are satisfactory you can now embark on the final delicate moulding. Different shades of the basic colour tones can help to indicate the folds of garments. Finally, give the hair a clear and attractive style. The king and queen should also be given their crowns, and some of the fairies arms and hands. Shape the hands beforehand and then lay them on.

11 Adding colour

21

12 Final details

The Star Thalers

The Star Thalers picture should be created on a dark blue background as the story takes place in the dark. This kind of motif is suitable for beginners. The action forms the centre of the picture. The forest only needs to be lightly indicated, so not every tree has to be detailed from top to bottom. The observer's imagination must also be given scope to fill out the picture.

It may be easier to make the stars on another piece of felt, and then add them to the picture, because if they have not turned out properly, and you have to take them off again you could damage your picture. The stars can be laid on as bright tufts, or as thin strips laid diagonally over each other.

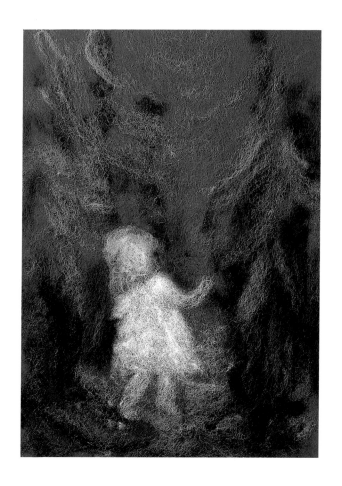

13 The basic composition

23

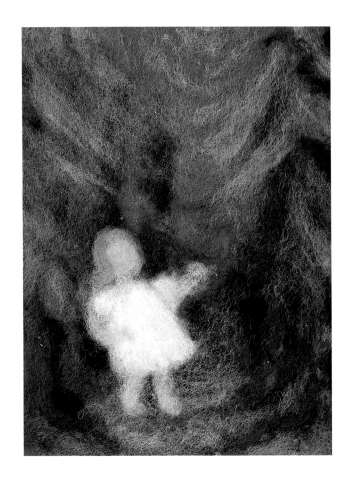

14 Adding colour

15 Adding stars and starlight

Rumpelstiltskin

This picture is determined on the one hand by the darkness out of which the messenger is watching from his hiding place, and on the other, by the bright fire around which the little man is dancing. Both parts of the picture are laid on a light blue background, and the forest floor and the leaves are created with different shades of colour.

Again the colours of the figures, the fire and the tree trunks can be intensified when you are happy with your composition. Under or between the green of the leaves the light-coloured felt is covered with dark blue wool, so that it shows up more brightly when lit by the fire.

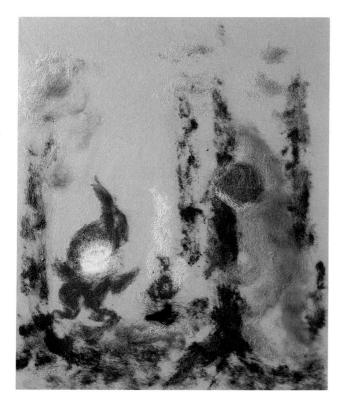

16 The basic composition

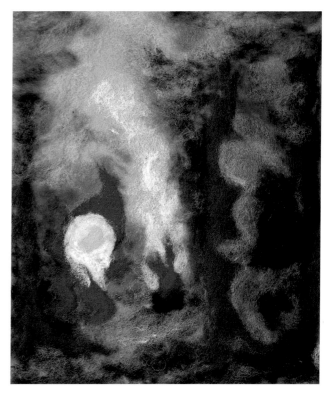

17 Adding colour

It is night-time and the fire is flickering brightly, so if the relationship between forms and colours is balanced, you can now emphasise the contrasts between light and dark. You can see how lighter and darker sections have been added to the figures and trees as highlights and shadows.

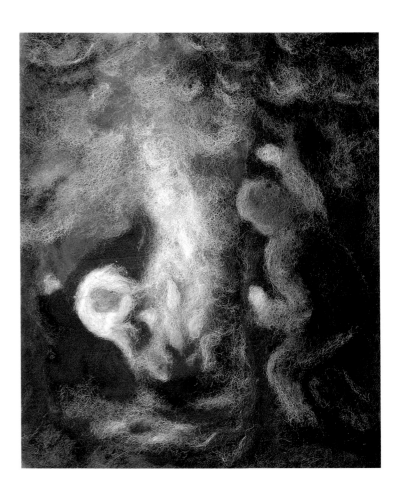

18 Adding highlights and shadows

Snow White and Rose Red

The light blue felt underlay is still visible in the middle of this picture. The dark surround frames the space in the centre of the picture, and red suggests that the figures are next to a fire. The mother, the little dove and the lamb are watching what the children are doing; it is an intimate scene of togetherness.

19 Snow White and Rose Red

Cinderella

Dark brown felt is the base for this picture. The window is covered with several very thin layers of white wool until no more of the dark background shines through. It is then firmly ironed flat. By doing this, the yellow and blue which are then laid on top have more lustre. The wall is created from various red, blue and brown shades; here, the brown of the underlay can remain visible. The doves can be made on an extra piece of felt before being brought to their final place on the finished background. In this picture, try to capture different movements. Everything is grouped round the little pot in which the good peas or lentils are collected.

20 Cinderella

Saint Christopher

Again it is night-time, so the base colour is dark blue. Christopher and the child should be completed first, and then the water laid on top. The circle of light around the child reminds us that Christopher feels as if he is carrying the whole world.

21 Saint Christopher

The Christmas Rose (by Selma Lagerlöf)

In this picture both the abbot and Robber Mother have their backs to the observer, guiding the viewer to experience the miracle of the Holy Night with them in the forest. The blossom of the flowers and the leaves growing on the trees are only gently suggested by the colours.

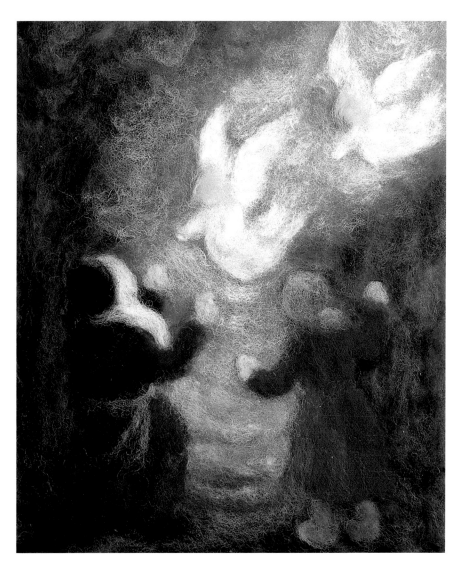

22 The Christmas Rose

The shepherd

The picture of a shepherd portrays a well-known and versatile scene, to which you can create simple stories. He watches over his sheep in all weathers. Make the animals quite distinct in the foreground. It is best to use uncarded washed fleece for this. In the background smaller and smaller irregular lumps of wool indicate the rest of a large flock. In this way the imagination is stimulated to fill out the picture, and think about what may lie beyond the scene depicted. The base of this picture is beige.

23 The shepherd

Children playing

This scene of children playing also portrays a common situation from daily life to which you can create simple stories. Here the light blue base is still visible in the sky.

24 Children playing

The Little Donkey

In this picture the meeting between the princess and the little donkey is brought right into the foreground. A rose bush can be included on the left. The cheerful, sunny mood of the palace garden is reflected by bright, airy colours on a beige background.

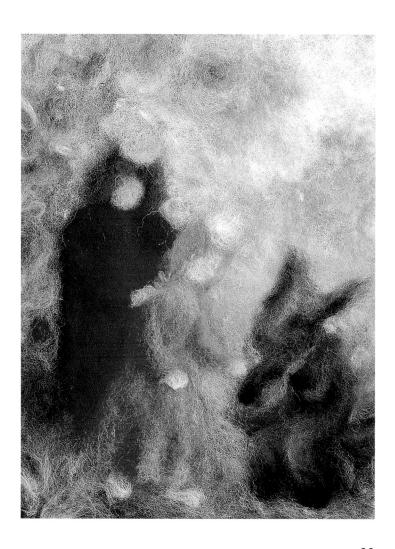

25 The Little Donkey

The Frog Prince

The focus of this picture is the meeting between the frog prince and the princess. The setting is left unclear, with a suggestion of a path and a palace, so that viewers can imagine the fairy-tale world for themselves. A light blue background has been used.

26 The Frog Prince

Saint Francis

In this picture the light blue base is covered with a little lightly-coloured wool, and is still easily visible. The birds flock together in all sizes around the saint, and can be created in all kinds of positions to indicate movement. They are teased out from white wool so that they stand out clearly from the foreground, and the unity of the picture is maintained. At the end, some of the birds could be given slightly different shading by using a few strands of coloured wool.

27 Saint Francis preaching to the birds

Three angels

In this picture a light yellow base is covered with darker shades of yellow to make a luminous background. Using different shades of blue will add movement, texture and highlights to the angels' robes.

28 Three angels (after Stefan Lochner)

The flight into Egypt

Here the dark blue felt base provides the colour for the sky, which is barely covered with wool, and darkened towards the top. The donkey should emerge first from the background, after being partially underlaid with a dark colour. This produces a shadow and is especially noticeable at the legs.

29 The flight into Egypt

Figures

The initial stages of making the figures and animals shown in the pictures are described in detail to begin with. Don't skip these instructions as you will need them for making the figures described further on.

MATERIALS
Unspun sheep's wool
Scissors
A long, thin sewing needle
Coloured wool yarn
A thick and a thin crochet hook

Dolls

The little woollen dolls shown in Figure 30 were produced with practically no aids. You just need unspun wool and a little skill with your hands. Nevertheless, a long thin sewing needle, thread and a crochet hook can be useful: one to secure the ends of the wool, and the other for pulling the wool in.

For this, hanks of wool, which have been carded and rolled into thick balls, are most suitable. This wool is more easily worked than

30 Woollen dolls

fleece wool, which can also be used. The dolls shown each need 40 cm (16 in) strands; their final height is 15 cm (6 in).

Divide the strands in two by tying a knot to create not quite equal lengths on either side of the knot (see Figure 31). The difference in length should be about 3 cm (1 in). The knot will later become the head. Hold the knotted strand vertically with the longer end at the top and the strands of the knot running horizontally. Bend the top part of the wool down and round the knot leaving the face free in front (see Figure 32). Tie a strand of wool below the knot to create the head.

If you have wound this last strand of wool firmly you will not need to sew it up. In this way a neck at least 1 cm ($1/2$ in) long will have been created. This is important because the wool clothes are quite bulky and the doll will look very chubby without a neck! For this reason, it is good if the head (knot) is made quite long.

Now divide some of the wool on either side to make arms. Use about $1/8$ of the total strands. Carefully lengthen these strands by about 3 cm (1 in), so that you can tie the ends after bending them into the waist (see Figures 33 and 34). You can loosely tie off these bits. If you add a wool strand from the waist to the feet of the doll to make a skirt, and then secure it, the doll will stand securely.

Compare the arm lengths and begin to wind wool for the clothes round. Choose coloured wool for the garments. You can also begin at the wrists or at the belt or at the neck (the hands remain unclothed). By winding the wool crosswise over the breast and back you can adjust the position of the arms by pulling the wool more or less tightly. Do not let the wool twist while this is being done. Sometimes it is easier not to wind the wool round the doll but to hold your hand still with the wool and twist the doll round the wool.

For the skirt, pull the wool flat apart into a square of the required size. Put the top edge round a double yarn and tie the whole thing

31 and 32 Making the head

firmly at the waist, with the right side facing out.

Finally lay the hair round the head. As the dolls are made for children to play with, it is recommended that vulnerable places are secured with little stitches. They will be hardly visible if they follow the same direction as the rest of the wool (see Figures 33 and 34).

33 and 34 Tying up the neck; dividing and bending the arms

An alternative simple way of making dolls is as follows:

Take a tuft of white wool, draw it out and lay it in a double thickness. Then, lay a ball of wool in the middle, and make a nice round head by wrapping the tuft of wool round the ball. Then tie off the neck with a thread drawn from the body.

Tease out some wool for the arms from both sides of the wool below the head. Tie off the wrists and waist again with a thread from the main tuft of wool.

For the dress, first make a hole in a finely teased-out coloured piece of wool, and push the doll's head through the hole. Press the coloured wool closely round the whole figure and hold it in place in the middle with a loose girdle.

Alternatively, if the body is made from coloured wool it can serve as a dress at the same time. In this case tease out more thinly the white column with the head which has already been made, and wrap it round below the head with a coloured wool fleece, for the full length of the body. It can be secured at the neck with a little thread.

The arms are again teased out sideways, and you can insert a white tuft of wool for the hands, before tying up the wrists.

For the hair thinly tease out a little wool and lay it round the head.

35 Dolls made using an alternative method

Gnomes

Knot a 20 cm (4 in) long wool strand, as described for the dolls (see Figures 31 and 32). The length of the neck is not important this time. What does matter is that the head, which is relatively large and covered with a pointed cap, rests on a little body, and that the long beard is clearly visible.

Lay the beard as a strand over the head and knot it under the chin.

The little coloured cloak is also laid over the head from one side to the other, and is fastened round the neck and under the beard. Then the point of the cap can easily be drawn upwards.

Finally some stitches will help to make the knot of the beard disappear.

36 Gnomes

42

A farmer

The farmer is formed from two 50 cm (20 in) long strands of wool and made in the same way as the dolls (pages 38–40).

He also wears a skirt, and the line of the belt is hidden by a long smock. The brown cloak is hung on a thread round his neck, and secured like the skirt.

The hair and beard are sewn on with a few stitches before the hat is put on. The brim of the hat consists of a strand laid round the head and secured.

As the hands consist of loops you can pull the sack through and up easily with a crochet hook. Use a rough twig for his walking stick. Before inserting it through the hand, cover the twig with adhesive tape to avoid it catching. This can be removed afterwards.

37 A farmer

Animals

Larger animals need a wire frame to be able to stand. Wire covered with string is thick and very stable, but not so flexible as pipe-cleaners. Normal pipe-cleaners are suitable for small animals. For larger ones, try to find extra long pipe-cleaners, or twist the ends of two together to make one long one.

Start with a little sheep. This is not so big, and if it does not turn out perfectly, it will not be so noticeable in the flock which is to follow. Take pipe-cleaners for the little sheep and bend them as shown in Figure 38 and 39. The legs and back should be the same length. The legs will later become shorter as the back is more thickly wrapped. The doubled wire is bent in such a way that the looped ends become the toes. The legs should be fixed to the wire on the sheep's back, so that later when the wool is wrapped round they do not slip.

When wrapping the wool, begin at the legs by drawing a very small end of a narrow strand of wool, about 40 cm (16 in) long, through the wires. Wrap this two to three times round the lowest wire loop then squeeze the two wires together and wrap them as described for the dolls (see pages 38–40). Secure all the wool strands from the legs to the sheep's back before starting on the back itself, which is done beginning at the tail.

Wrap some wool round the wire for the head then bend the wire forward to form a head shape (see Figure 39). Add more wool as required to make a good head shape. The hindquarters should also be formed in this way.

Finally, lay loose wool on for the fleece and secure it with widely spaced little stitches.

Make the ears individually by twisting some wool with a crochet hook. Push the hook into the back and out at the head, drawing the wool through. You can also pull some wool with a thick needle through the head from one side to the other, and tease each protruding end into an ear shape.

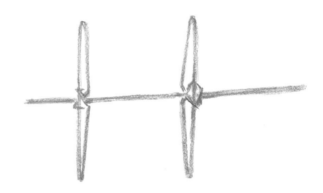

38 Basic wire frame for animals

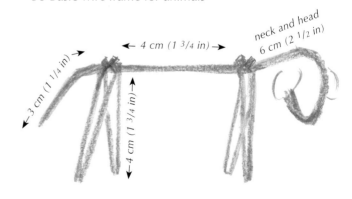

39 Measurements for a sheep; shaping the head

Animals for The Little Palace

The animals made here can also be used for the puppet story described on pages 62–64.

For the *midge* knot a small strand of wool and tease out little wings from the two ends sticking out of the knot.

Make the *fly* in exactly the same way, but a little bigger and in a different colour.

For the *mouse* use a pipe-cleaner. Wrap it first with wool and then bend it into the shape shown in Figure 40, pressing the wire together in front at the nose. Then wrap the mouse up tightly with unspun wool. Towards the rear, you can bridge the wider gap in the wire frame with figure-of-eight loops (Figure 41). Then wrap across from the hindquarters and behind the head using a crochet hook through the wool (Figure 42). As with the sheep, the ears consist of wool loops, but this time standing upright. The tail is twisted. If you want to give the mouse legs, pull out two wires and wrap them with wool.

For the *frog*, loop a 50 cm (20 in) wire, to make a frame for the body and hind legs (see Figure 43). Also make two legs about 9 cm (3 3/4 in) long, as shown in Figure 44. Wrap each foot separately then bind the frames together with wool before working further on the legs (see Figure 45). Fill the body in a similar way to that of the mouse. When everything is finished you can sew on bright eyes, which look more friendly than dark ones.

The little *hare* can easily be made without a frame. Roll a square piece of wool from the

40 Mouse frame

41 Wrapping the mouse

42 Wrapping the mouse

fleece into a longish shape, rounded at both ends, which represents the body, and secure them at the bottom with a few stitches. At one end tie off the head with a thin thread which should if possible be invisible. Make the ears as with the little sheep.

The *fox* and the *wolf* are made with similar frames to the sheep (see page 44).

Because the *bear* is a big animal it demands more skill and patience, but as soon as it is wrapped up stably you can shape the dark wool which covers him. For reinforcement his head should have more wire inside than the other animals.

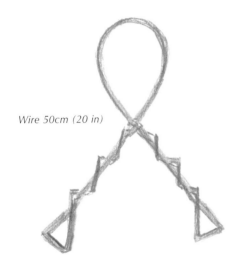

Wire 50cm (20 in)

43 Main frog frame

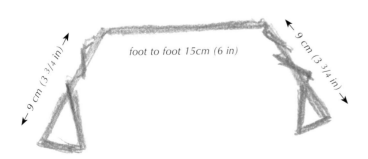

9 cm (3 3/4 in) *foot to foot 15cm (6 in)* *9 cm (3 3/4 in)*

44 Frog's legs

45 Final frog shape

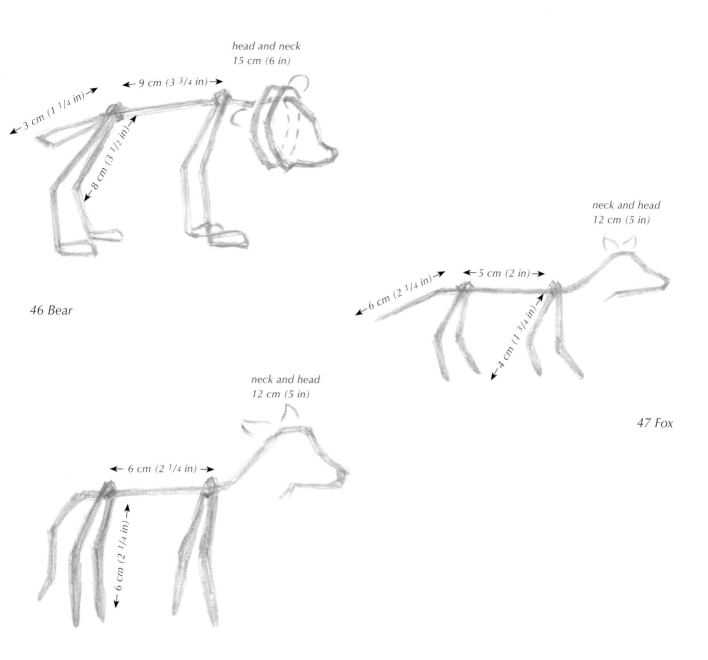

head and neck
15 cm (6 in)

← 9 cm (3 3/4 in) →

← 3 cm (1 1/4 in) →

8 cm (3 1/2 in)

46 Bear

neck and head
12 cm (5 in)

← 6 cm (2 1/4 in) →

← 5 cm (2 in) →

4 cm (1 3/4 in)

47 Fox

neck and head
12 cm (5 in)

← 6 cm (2 1/4 in) →

6 cm (2 1/4 in)

48 Wolf

Birds

Begin as if you were making a doll (see page 38–40). Behind the knot, tie up the head without creating a neck. For the wings, divide more wool than for the doll's arms. The body, which is only a little bigger than the head is tied at the read end. Tease out the tail and the wings. For the beak, pull some wool out of the head, or sew a beak on with different coloured wool.

An alternative way of making birds is as follows:

Take a small strand of wool about 20 cm (8 in) long, double it and then knot it in such a way

49 Little birds

48

that the knot becomes the body. At one end the tail sticks out and at the other the remaining loop makes the head. Here again, the wool is drawn out to make the beak. Pull a strand of wool through the body (knot) with a crochet hook or thick darning needle, so that it sticks out at both sides and can be loosely teased into wings.

50 Alternative bird method

Crib figures

It is better not to make crib figures in the presence of children, so that the nativity scene can appear as a kind of revelation. The figures stand on little wooden discs about 5 cm (2 in) in diameter. Drill a little hole in the middle to take a wooden rod or pencil. Sharpen the top with a pencil sharpener (see figure 51). The height should be about 3–4 cm (1 1/2 in) shorter than the crib figures. The figures are then made in the same way as the dolls already described (see pages 38–40). Once the neck has been wrapped, push the rod from below so that it reaches into the neck. Secure all the wool to the wood with the waistband.

The skirts of all the figures are also secured with a strand of wool. Carefully draw the coloured wool apart and lay it like a piece of cloth round the figure. The clothing should be as thin as possible, and can be tied round the base of the rod. This also improves the appearance of the figure.

The arms of the *angel* remain loose and are not wrapped, only the hands are lightly tied off. Sew the wings, made from a single strand of wool, between the shoulders. The angel should have a light, airy effect.

Mary is a little smaller than Joseph, and so the strand of wool to be knotted is a little shorter than that of all the other figures, by about 5–6 cm (2 in). Wrap the arms with the red wool of the robe up to the shoulders. Secure the robe itself round the neck as with the doll's skirt and pull the arms through on each side. After laying hair round the face lay the blue cloak round the whole figure.

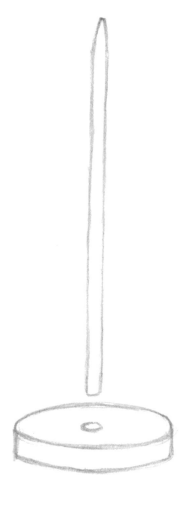

51 Wooden stand for crib figures

If necessary, sew it to the head and wrists with some loose stitches that are hardly visible on the outside.

Joseph has a brown undergarment and a reddish coloured cloak with a collar or hood. Sew the grey hair and beard on with a few stitches.

For the *child* use only one kind of light-coloured wool. The child does not have to be dressed. Keep the neck short, and tie up the hands lightly. The arms are not wrapped. Below the feet turn the wool up and back so that it looks like a little sack. Begin winding a long thin strand of wool under the arms, first down towards the feet to secure the end of the strand, then back up and across the chest and over the back. Draw the last end of the strand inside with a crochet hook

52 Shepherds at the crib

(see figure 54). The whole thing holds together without a knot.

Make the *shepherds* in the same way as the farmer (see page 43). You can also hang a 'sheepskin' round them.

The *kings* wear long robes. Dress their wrapped arms with more loose wool which hangs down.

The way to make the *ox* and the *ass* is shown in the figures 55 and 56. The method is described on page 44.

53 Kings at the crib

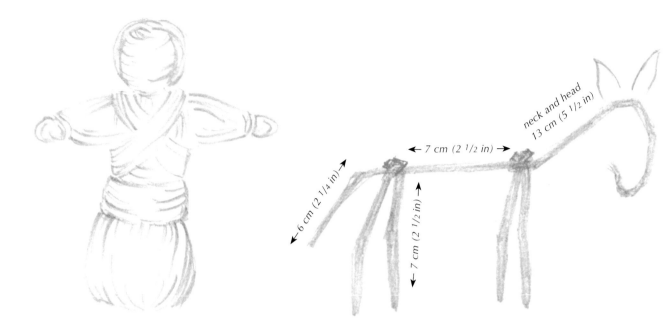

54 Wrapping the child

neck and head
13 cm (5 1/2 in)

← 7 cm (2 1/2 in) →

← 6 cm (2 1/4 in) →

← 7 cm (2 1/2 in) →

55 Donkey

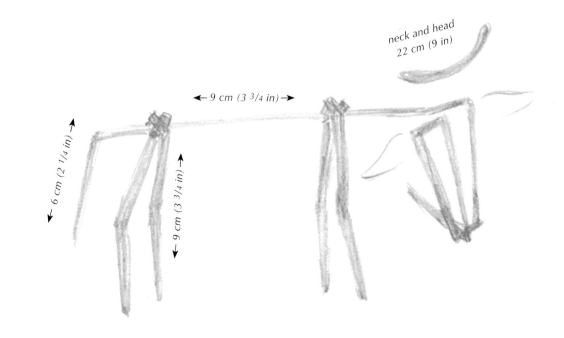

neck and head
22 cm (9 in)

← 9 cm (3 3/4 in) →

← 6 cm (2 1/4 in) →

← 9 cm (3 3/4 in) →

56 Ox

53

Using Unspun Wool in Kindergartens

by Freya Jaffke

Raw wool

Unspun sheep's wool is an indispensable material in Waldorf kindergartens. Not only is it suitable for making dolls and puppets, stuffing dolls' beds and toy cushions, but also for all kinds of play and making shapes. When delicately teased out it can be laid as a carpet in the room of a homemade dolls' house; skilful six-year-old children can make artistic hairstyles for their rag dolls; loose tufts can be used to make gnomes with beards; it can decorate the branches, cones and twigs of trees with leaves and snow; or it can rise as smoke from houses in hollow tree trunks.

It is wonderful if you manage to get a sack of wool from a freshly-shorn sheep. What a multiplicity of enlivening sense impressions are evoked! Children happily plunge their hands into such a soft, slightly greasy, yellow-white-brown coloured mountain of wool, which still smells of the sheep. Generally it needs to be washed in a big washtub, then rinsed and spread out to dry. It takes several days before the wool has dried completely, and can be used.

Teasing and carding wool

Usually wool needs to be teased out carefully. Wool should not be torn apart, but carefully teased out with the fingertips. This activity helps to develop gentleness in children.

If the wool is to be used as stuffing, for dolls' beds or toy cushions, it can be carded with hand-carders. The clumps are then combed out as long strands, which lie well together and do not matt so quickly when used.

To obtain finer and more beautiful wool, use two carders with fine teeth, which allow the wool to be properly combed out (see Figures 57 to 61).

One board should be laid on your knee, and clumps evenly placed lengthwise (Figure 57).

Then stroke the other board over the first board, gently at first, then more strongly, and alternately to the left (Figure 58) and right (Figure 59).

Once all the clumps have been carded, the wool can be pulled off by stroking in the opposite direction – it comes off as a fluffy roll (Figures 60 and 61).

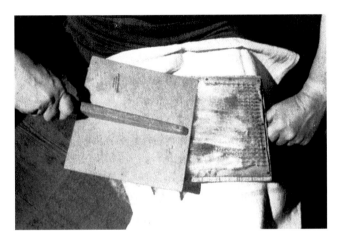

58

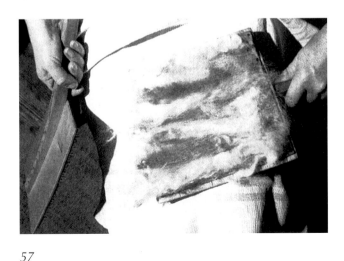

57

59

As this activity requires certain skill and strength, it is difficult for children to do, but it might be possible using small children's carders.

60

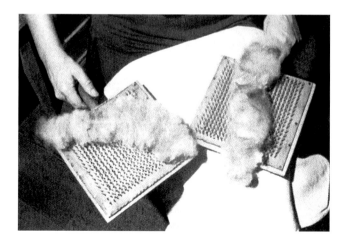

61

Dyeing wool

You can also dye wool using natural dyes. There are many books on the subject, which explain the process in great detail. It is an enjoyable and rewarding process, which I have explained briefly below, but you will need to find further information if you would like to try dyeing wool yourself.

Wash the wool to remove dirt and grease. Most pant dyes require a mordant, such as alum, copper sulphate or ferrous sulphate, which helps to fix the colours. Check in detail which mordant to use with which plant dyes. The dyeing is done by boiling the wool, to which the mordant has already been applied, in a dye bath made of tea leaves, onion skins, lichens, plant leaves or even blossom.

The process is very exciting as the final colour is often quite different from how it looked in the dye bath. Children may have suggestions for which blossoms to use to make special colours.

Using magic wool creatively with children

No matter what you make with wool, children will want to join in. Arrange the different colours of wool in a basket as this helps impress a sense of beauty and order on children. A basket especially for them also allows them to copy without disturbing your basket. From their own basket they can take what they wish, and following your example, they will usually only take a little at a time and work very carefully with it. Leave the children quite free – some will copy the work of the adult, while others will create things out of their own imagination. Allow them free scope in their eager, and often very original, activity.

Although children of pre-school age sometimes like to copy a wool picture, they often prefer to model. Indeed, it is a characteristic of children of that age that they can hardly pass a sandpit or a tub of clay without enthusiastically putting their hands into it and starting to make something.

62 Coloured wool

A modelled landscape

From coloured wool you can create a built-up landscape. Lay a cloth on a table as an underlay. To ensure the landscape will not slip, do not hang it over the edge of the table.

Use a thinly teased tuft of blue wool to make a lake in the middle, on which lots of little yellow and white ducks or swans can swim. These are indicated by small tufts of wool. The children can find twigs which can be stuck into wooden discs, and hung with thin wisps of wool to make trees. Out of the lake there flows a river, on which a little woollen boat is floating. In the meadow by the river is a shepherd with his flock of sheep, surrounded by little bushes and trees. In one corner make a farmhouse, adding a stable and a kennel made of little bits of wood, all for the farmer and his family.

This scene is not meant to be permanent, but at the end of the day can be carefully taken apart, to make way for new ideas and impulses on the next day.

To ensure that modelling with coloured wool remains a special activity, don't let it become a daily occurrence in a kindergarten.

63 A modelled landscape

A table puppet show

You can make figures for a table puppet show with the children. Make the figures as described earlier (see pages 38–40 for people and pages 44–47 for animals). Once their interest has been aroused, the children will join in and make the most beautiful and original forms. Four to five-year-old children are usually soon finished; they are quite undemanding as far as the recognizable form is concerned, for their imagination does all the rest. Six or seven-year-olds, on the other hand, become engrossed in this activity and show concentration and patience. They also observe carefully what the grown-up is doing.

It is important to choose a characteristic colour for each animal, and only to create the animal's essential shape, omitting detail and differentiation. Allow the children complete freedom in choosing other colours. In this way their imagination is stimulated.

Once all the figures are finished and the cloths and other bits and pieces are ready, you can start building up a little story.

64 Scene for a table puppet show

Children are usually keen to help build a home for each animal. In *The Little Palace*, for example, the Midge and the Fly live in a tree, the Frog by a little lake, the Mouse in a hole, the Fox in a den, and so on. In the middle you can lay a yellow-brown cloth in the shape of a bowl (see Figure 64). It must be big enough for all the animals to find room in it. Don't worry that the 'earthenware pot' on which all the animals knock is open at the top, or that it is much larger than the one which fell off the farmer's cart as he was passing along!

At the first telling, only the adult should move the figures, but the next day some of the children can join in and help to move the animals, but the adult should tell the story. Although the story appears to lend itself to giving different speakers individual parts, it is better to allow the children to be absorbed by the story simply through listening and watching.

In some kindergartens this play has been performed daily for a whole week at a time, building up the scene afresh during free-play

65 The Little Palace

time. During the last days the five and six-year-old children would do this by themselves. At the same time other children, alone or in groups, would make their own picture, and all the time you could hear bits of the story with the children giving the animals wonderful names. For animals the children would use little carved pieces of wood, a coloured rolled-up bit of wool, or a knotted handkerchief.

If a puppet play is introduced into the daily activity of the kindergarten in this way, it will have a much more stimulating effect on the play of the children than if the completed scene suddenly appears.

Here is a suitable story to use:

THE LITTLE PALACE

A farmer was taking some earthenware pots to market when one fell off his cart.

Along came Fly Buzzy-Buzz, who asked, 'Whose is this little house, this little palace? Who lives here?'

Nobody answered; the house was empty. So in flew the Fly and he settled there.

Soon along came Midge Sing-So-Fine, who asked, 'Whose is this little house? Who lives in the palace, in the little palace?'

'I live here, I am Fly Buzzy-Buzz and who are you?'

'I am Midge Sing-So-Fine.'

'Come and live with me.'

So the two of them lived together.

Then along came Little Mouse Nibble-Nobble, who asked, 'Whose is this little house? Who lives in the palace, the little palace?'

'I am Fly Buzzy-Buzz and I am Midge Sing-So-Fine, and who are you?'

'I am Little Mouse Nibble-Nobble.'

'If you like you can come and live with us.'

So all three lived together.

Then Frog Croakety-Croak came hopping along. 'Whose is the little house? Who lives in the palace, in the little palace?'

'I am Fly Buzzy-Buzz, and I am Midge Sing-So-Fine, and I am Little Mouse Nibble-Nobble, and who are you?'

'I am Frog Croakety-Croak.'

'If you like you can come and live with us.'

So now all four lived together.

A little hare now came hopping along.

'Whose is this little house? Who lives in the palace, in the little palace?'

'I am Fly Buzzy-Buzz, and I am Midge Sing-So-Fine, and I am Little Mouse Nibble-Nobble, and I am frog Croakety-Croak, and who are you?'

'I am Little Hare Hoppety-Hop.'

'If you like you can live with us.'

So now all five lived together.

Then a fox came along and asked, 'Whose is the little house? Who lives in the palace, the little palace?'

'I am Fly Buzzy-Buzz, I am Midge Sing-So-Fine, I am Little Mouse Nibble-Nobble, I am Frog Croakety-Croak, I am Little Hare Hoppety-Hop, and who are you?'

'I am Red Fox Yap-a-Lot.'

'If you like you can come and live with us.'

So now all six lived together.

Then along came a wolf. 'Whose is the little house? Who lives in the palace, the little palace?'

'I am Fly Buzzy-Buzz, I am Midge Sing-So-Fine, I am Little Mouse Nibble-Nobble, I am Frog Croakety-Croak, I am Little Hare Hoppety-Hop, I am Red Fox Yap-a-Lot, and who are you?'

'I am Wild Wolf Howl-at-the-Moon.'

'If you like you can come and live with us.'

So now all seven lived together.

Then along came a bear.

'Whose is this little house? Who lives in the palace, in the little palace?'

'I am Fly Buzzy-Buzz, I am Midge Sing-So-Fine, I am Little Mouse Nibble-Nobble, I am Frog Croakety-Croak, I am Little Hare Hoppety-Hop, I am Fox Yap-a-Lot, I am Wild Wolf Howl-at-the-Moon, and who are you?'

'I am Bear Hugging-Paws.'

'If you like you can come and live with us.'

The Bear seized the pot with his paws and he hugged it so hard that it broke and all the animals fell out and started to run away. First, Bear Hugging-Paws, then Wild Wolf Howl-at-the-Moon, then Red Fox Yap-a-Lot, then Little Hare Hoppety-Hop, then Frog Croakety-Croak, then Little Mouse Nibble-Nobble, then Midge Sing-So-Fine, then Fly Buzzy-Buzz.

Further reading

Adolphi, Sybille, *Making Fairy Tale Scenes,* Floris Books, Edinburgh.

—, *Making Flower Children,* Floris Books, Edinburgh

—, *Making More Flower Children,* Floris Books, Edinburgh.

Anschütz, Marieke, *Children and their Temperaments,* Floris Books, Edinburgh.

Barz, Brigitte, *Festivals with Children,* Floris Books, Edinburgh.

Berger, Petra, *Feltcraft,* Floris Books, Edinburgh.

Berger, Thomas, *The Christmas Craft Book,* Floris Books, Edinburgh.

Berger, Thomas & Petra, *Crafts through the Year,* Floris Books, Edinburgh.

—, *The Gnome Craft Book,* Floris Books, Edinburgh.

Clouder, Chris & Martyn Rawson, *Waldorf Education,* Floris Books, Edinburgh.

Crossley, Diana, *Muddles, Puddles and Sunshine,* Hawthorn Press, Stroud.

Dancy, Rahima Baldwin, *You are your Child's First Teacher,* Hawthorn Press, Stroud.

Evans, Russell, *Helping Children to Overcome Fear,* Hawthorn Press, Stroud.

Guéret, Frédérique, *Magical Window Stars,* Floris Books, Edinburgh.

Jaffke, Freya, *Work and Play in Early Childhood,* Floris Books, Edinburgh & Anthroposophic Press, New York.

—, *Celebrating Festivals with Children,* Floris Books, Edinburgh.

Jenkinson, Sally, *The Genius of Play,* Hawthorn Press, Stroud.

König, Karl, *The First Three Years of the Child,* Floris Books, Edinburgh.

Kornberger, Horst, *The Power of Stories,* Floris Books, Edinburgh.

Kutsch, Irmgard and Brigitte Walden, *Spring Nature Activities for Children,* Floris Books, Edinburgh.

—, *Summer Nature Activities for Children,* Floris Books, Edinburgh.

—, *Autumn Nature Activities for Children,* Floris Books, Edinburgh.

—, *Winter Nature Activities for Chidren,* Floris Books, Edinburgh.

Kraul, Walter, *Earth, Water, Fire and Air,* Floris Books, Edinburgh.

Leeuwen, M van & J Moeskops, *The Nature Corner,* Floris Books, Edinburgh.

Mellon, Nancy, *Storytelling with Children,* Hawthorn Press, Stroud.

Meyer, Rudolf, *The Wisdom of Fairy Tales,* Floris Books, Edinburgh.

Müller, Brunhild, *Painting with Children,* Floris Books, Edinburgh.

Neuschütz, Karin, *Sewing Dolls,* Floris Books, Edinburgh.

—, *Creative Wool*, Floris Books, Edinburgh.

Oldfield, Lynne, *Free to Learn,* Hawthorn Press, Stroud.

Petrash, Carol, *Earthwise: Environmental Crafts and Activities with Young Children*, Floris Books, Edinburgh & Gryphon House, Maryland.

Rawson, Martyn & Michael Rose, *Ready to Learn,* Hawthorn Press, Stroud.

Reinhard, Rotraud, *A Felt Farm*, Floris Books, Edinburgh.

Reinckens, Sunnhild, *Making Dolls,* Floris Books, Edinburgh.

Santer, Ivor, *Green Fingers and Muddy Boots,* Floris Books, Edinburgh.

Sealey, Maricristin, *Kinder Dolls,* Hawthorn Press, Stroud.

Steiner, Rudolf, *The Education of the Child in the Light of Anthroposophy,* Steiner Press, London, & Anthroposophic Press, New York.

Taylor, Michael, *Finger Strings,* Floris Books, Edinburgh.

Thomas, Anne & Peter, *The Children's Party Book,* Floris Books, Edinburgh

Wolck-Gerche, Angelika, *Creative Felt,* Floris Books, Edinburgh.

—, *More Magic Wool,* Floris Books, Edinburgh.

—, *Papercraft,* Floris Books, Edinburgh.

Resources

SOURCES FOR MAGIC WOOL AND NATURAL MATERIALS

AUSTRALIA
Morning Star
www.morningstarcrafts.com.au

Winterwood Toys
www.winterwoodtoys.com.au

NORTH AMERICA
The Waldorf Early Childhood Association of North America maintains an online list of suppliers at: www.waldorfearlychildhood.org/sources.asp

UK
Myriad Natural Toys
www.myriadonline.co.uk

WALDORF SCHOOLS

Waldorf schools and kindergartens are found in over 60 countries around the world. Up-to-date information can be found on any of the websites below.

AUSTRALIA
Association of Rudolf Steiner Schools in Australia, PO Box 111, Robertson, NSW 2577
rssa@bigpond.com
www.steineroz.com

NEW ZEALAND
Federation of Rudolf Steiner Schools, PO Box 888, Hastings, Hawkes Bay
waldorf@voyager.nz
www.rudolfsteinerfederation.org.nz

NORTH AMERICA
Association of Waldorf Schools of North America, 3911 Bannister Road, Fair Oaks, CA 95628
awsna@awsna.org
www.whywaldorfworks.org

SOUTH AFRICA
Southern African Federation of Waldorf Schools, PO Box 280, Plumstead 7801
federation@waldorf.org.za
www.waldorf.org.za

UK
Steiner Schools Fellowship, Kidbrooke Park, Forest Row, RH18 5JB
mail@swsf.org.uk
www.steinerwaldorf.org.uk

Thomas and Petra Berger
ISBN 978–086315–827–8

Petra Berger
ISBN 978–086315–720–2

Karin Neuschütz
ISBN 978–086315–800–1

Angelika Wolk-Gerche
ISBN 978–086315–678–6

www.florisbooks.co.uk

Toymaking with Children

Freya Jaffke

Freya Jaffke
ISBN 978–086315–769–1

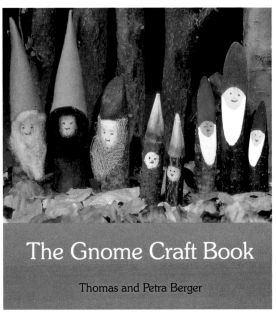

The Gnome Craft Book

Thomas and Petra Berger

Thomas and Petra Berger
ISBN 978–086315–721–9

The Nature Corner

Celebrating the year's cycle with seasonal tableaux

M. van Leeuwen and J. Moeskops

M. Van Leeuwen and J. Moeskops
ISBN 978–086315–721–9

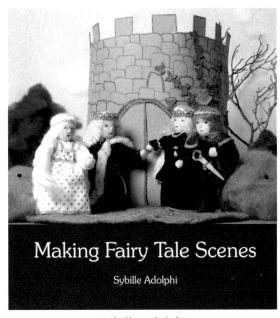

Making Fairy Tale Scenes

Sybille Adolphi

Sybille Adolphi
ISBN 978–086315–718–9

www.florisbooks.co.uk

Sybille Adolphi
ISBN 978–086315–650–2

Sybille Adolphi
ISBN 978–086315–685–4

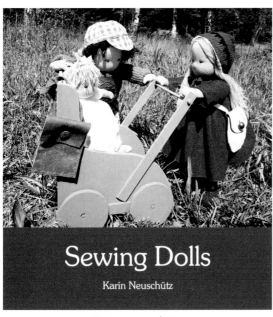

Karin Neuschütz
ISBN 978–086315–719–6

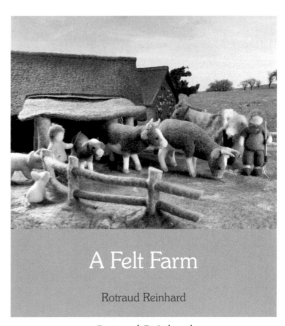

Rotraud Reinhard
ISBN 978–086315–789–9

www.florisbooks.co.uk

Irmgard Kutsch & Brigitte Walden
ISBN 978–086315–544–4

Irmgard Kutsch & Brigitte Walden
ISBN 978–086315–586–4

Irmgard Kutsch & Brigitte Walden
ISBN 978–086315–495–9

Irmgard Kutsch & Brigitte Walden
ISBN 978–086315–564–2

www.florisbooks.co.uk